PRAISE for *Overview of the Bible for Babes in Christ*

"Clear and Simple"

"…I want to share my honest experience. I've just given my life to Jesus Christ, and as a new believer this is such an important season for me. This book came at the perfect time— it helped me not only understand the Bible, but also made it feel less overwhelming. I really appreciated how the author broke things down, summarizing both Old and New Testament in a way that was clear and simple. Each summary gave me a better grasp of what God's Word means, and it made reading the Bible feel easier and more enjoyable. I've already learned so much through it. I'd definitely recommend this book to other new believers who want to grow in their faith. For me, it's a five-star read."

—Christy, new believer

"An Engaging and Informative Read"

"The author does an amazing job of presenting the Bible in such a way that you are encouraged to explore the Word for yourself, showcasing the true warm and inviting nature of the Bible. 10 out of 10 - a great starting place for those curious or new to the faith while also being a great reintroduction for those in the faith looking to reignite their biblical learning."

—Marcus, believer

Overview of the Bible for Babes in Christ

Eileen J. Alsina, M.Ed.

EJA Endeavors
Moreno Valley, CA

Copyright Page for

Overview of the Bible for Babes in Christ

© 2025 Eileen Alsina/EJA Endeavors

Cover design by EJA Endeavors
"Babes in Christ" logo by Omar J. Williams

First Edition

ISBN: 979-8-9998048-0-8

Published by EJA Endeavors
alsinaej@icloud.com

Printed in the United States of America

Contents

Dedication

To the new believer —

The one who's curious, the one who's seeking, the one who's just beginning.

May this book be a light on your journey and a gentle reminder that God meets you right where you are.

You are seen. You are loved. You are never alone.

—

And to my children and grandchildren

You are my daily inspiration. Your lives, your questions, and your faith journeys have shaped this work more than you know.

I pray this legacy of love and truth will bless generations to come.

—Eileen

Introduction

Let me preface this book by saying I am not a Bible scholar. This book is not for Bible scholars; it is for anyone who has heard about Jesus Christ or recently accepted Jesus Christ as their Lord and Savior (became a Christian, or follower of Christ). My goal in writing this book, and others I plan to write, is simply to answer basic questions new Christians (Babes in Christ) may have.

I grew up in the Baptist Church. My grandfather was a pastor, or reverend as they were referred to back then. My grandmother was a devout Christian, instilling in my mother (Zerline) a love for Jesus Christ, which she passed on to her children, and I pray I have passed on to my children.

For years, I attended church because my mother took me. I was in my thirties when I recall hearing the senior pastor of the church I was attending say that I should read the Bible for myself. He said I should read it for myself to ensure that what he was telling me was true. It was an "ah ha" moment. Don't get me wrong, I had tried to read the Bible through the years, the King James version, but it just didn't make sense. Surely that was why we went to church—so the pastor would interpret it for us.

At this same church, I began teaching Youth Sunday School. During my study and preparation for the youth lessons, I realized just how much I didn't know about God, Jesus, and the Bible. How could I have been attending church for years and not know the basics about the God I serve? I admit, times were different then. We didn't have various Bible translations, if so, I didn't know about them. We didn't have the internet at our disposal, and I just didn't know what I didn't know.

I am ashamed to say that I was given this vision to write a series of books for Babes in Christ many years ago, but I let life be a distraction. Now that I think about it, perhaps it was life itself that has prepared me. My son recently reminded me of all the questions I had as a not-so-new Christian. In answering his questions, I was inspired to be obedient to what the Lord told me to do many years ago—simply answer some basic questions for Babes in Christ.

What is a "Babe in Christ?" In 1 Corinthians 3:1-2, Paul is writing to the Corinthian Church. He states, "Dear brothers and sisters, when I was with you, I couldn't talk to you as I would to spiritual people. I had to talk as though you belonged to this world or as though you were infants in Christ [Babes in Christ]. I had to feed you with milk, not solid food, because you weren't ready for anything stronger..." (NLT - New Living Translation).

In Ephesians 4:12-15, Paul again writes, "Their [the Church] responsibility is to equip God's people to do his work and build up the church, the body of Christ. This will continue until we all come to such unity in our faith and knowledge of God's Son that we will be mature in the Lord, measuring up to the full and complete standard of Christ. Then we will no longer be immature like children. We won't be tossed and blown about by every wind of new teaching. We will not be influenced when people try to trick us with lies so clever they sound like the truth. Instead, we will speak the truth in love, growing in every way more and more like Christ, who is the head of his body, the church," (NLT).

As a new Christian (Babe in Christ), you need milk, the basics. You are still an infant in your knowledge of Christ. I pray this book will be some of your milk, encouraging and enticing you to read the Bible. The more you study the Bible and learn, the more you mature to solid food—a deeper understanding and knowledge of God.

Overview

One of the most important things, I believe, for a new Christian, is to own a Bible. Not the one on your smartphone. A physical Bible. I may be old-fashioned, but there is something about holding the Bible in your hand, flipping the pages, searching for answers, reading scripture, and highlighting your favorite verses. As a Christian, the Bible is your foundation for living!

It is also important that you approach the Bible with an open mind and a willingness to learn. The Bible is a collection of books that were written over thousands of years, so it can be challenging to understand at first, but time and study will help shed light on various passages.

Additionally, remember that the Bible can be interpreted in different ways by different people. It will be helpful to seek commentaries and different translations to assist in deepening your understanding. I've listed a few commentaries and types of translations toward the end of the book.

One helpful approach to reading the Bible may be to start by reading the New Testament. The New Testament tells the story of Jesus, his teachings, his death, and his resurrection. The books of Matthew, Mark, Luke, and John provide accounts of Jesus' life. They are referred to as the Gospels, or "good news" from God.

Ultimately, the Bible is a guide for how to live a meaningful and fulfilling life. By studying and reflecting on Bible teachings, you will gain wisdom, guidance, and inspiration.

What is the Bible

What is the Bible? 2 Timothy 3:16-17 states, "All Scripture is inspired by God [God-breathed] and used to teach us what is true and to make us realize what is wrong in our lives. It corrects us when we are wrong and teaches us to do what is right. God uses it to prepare and equip his people to do every good work," (NLT). The Bible is the inspired words of God.

The Bible is divided into two main parts—the Old Testament, which contains thirty-nine books about God, and the New Testament, which consists of twenty-seven books about Jesus. The books contain chapters, just as a novel would; however, the Bible is different in that the chapter sentences are considered verses, and the verses are referred to as scripture, making it easy to direct someone to a location in the Bible.

The first book and line of the Bible for example: Genesis (book) 1:1 (chapter 1: verse 1) reads "In the beginning God created the heavens and the earth."

If I refer you to the scripture "Genesis 1:1" it would read: "In the beginning God created the heavens and the earth." Therefore, a scripture consists of a Book of the Bible (Genesis), the chapter (1), and the verse (1), or Book, chapter, verses– Genesis 1:1-2 "In the beginning God created the heavens and the earth. Now the earth was formless and empty, darkness was over the surface of the deep, and the Spirit of God was hovering over the waters," (NIV - New International Version).

Historical and Cultural Context

The Bible is a collection of religious texts that are sacred to Christians. The text contains stories, teachings, and guidance for believers of the Christian faith. Therefore, understanding the historical and cultural context of the Bible is important. Understanding the political and social climate of the time can help shed light on particular passages. This is where commentaries will be useful.

The historical context of the Bible is complex, as it covers over 2,000 years and includes many different cultures and civilizations. Understand that context is vital for interpreting the Bible's meaning. The cultures represented in the Bible include those of ancient Israel, Egypt, Greece, and Rome, among others.

These cultures had different beliefs, practices, and values, and these factors influenced the way the Bible was written and understood. For example, the ancient Israelites had a strong sense of community. They saw themselves as a chosen people with a special relationship with God. This influenced how they understood their history, laws, and religious practices. Similarly, the Greeks and Romans had unique perspectives on religion, philosophy, and politics, reflected in the New Testament writings. Understanding the cultural context of the Bible can help us better appreciate its message and relevance in today's world.

While the Bible does touch on political themes in some places, such as in the books of Kings and Chronicles, which describe the reigns of various kings, the primary focus of the Bible is on spiritual matters rather than political ones. That being said, there are undoubtedly political implications to some of the teachings and principles found in the Bible, such as the concepts of justice, mercy, and righteousness, which have been influential in shaping political systems throughout history.

Also, the social climate of the Bible was very different from what we experience today. The societies described in the Bible were primarily patriarchal, with men holding the majority of the power and women being viewed as subordinate. Slavery was also accepted as a normal part of life, and people of different races and cultures often faced discrimination and persecution. Despite these challenges and the differences in our social climate today, the Bible contains messages of love, compassion, and justice that continue to inspire people of faith today.

In the following pages, I have listed the books of the Bible with a short overview of each book, pointing out scriptures and some of my personal insights.

Old Testament

The Old Testament is the first part of the Christian Bible. It is a collection of religious texts and stories. It includes thirty-nine books that were written over a period of about 1,000 years, from around 1200 BCE (Before the Christian Era, or before the birth of Jesus Christ) to 165 BCE. These books contain stories describing the world's creation, the early history of humanity, and the relationship between God and his people. They also include laws and commandments, poetry and wisdom, literature, and prophecies about the future. The Old Testament is an integral part of the Christian faith. It serves as a foundation for understanding the teachings of Jesus Christ that are found in the New Testament.

Old Testament Books:

1. Genesis

Genesis is the first book listed in the Bible and tells the story of how God created the world and everything in it. It covers a lot of ground and contains stories you may have heard, including The Tower of Babel, The Flood, and The Creation of Adam and Eve. Throughout the book of Genesis, we see how God interacts with humanity and how humanity struggles to follow God's commands.

Genesis lays the foundation for many of the stories and beliefs central to the Christian and Jewish faiths. It includes the story of God's promise to Abraham to give him and his wife Sarah a son in their old age. God also promised that Abraham's descendants would be as numerous as the stars through the lineage of Abraham, his son Isaac, and Isaac's son Jacob.

Jacob stole his brother's birthright. Isaac's firstborn son was actually Esau. Read Genesis 27 through 35. It reads like a soap opera! It includes an account of Jacob wrestling with God. Afterward, Jacob was named Israel. His descendants are therefore referred to as Israelites.

Jacob had many sons. The youngest was Joseph. Jacob's beloved son Joseph was precious to his father but hated by his older brothers (read Genesis chapters 37-50). My family has an inside joke about Joseph. I have one son by birth, and my oldest daughter will often refer to him as "Joseph," meaning I'm treating him like he is my favorite. But he also will refer to her as "Joseph" when he feels I'm treating her special. It's cute, but unlike Jacob, I don't have a favorite son or daughter. I love all my beautiful children.

2. Exodus

Exodus tells the story of the Israelites' escape from slavery in Egypt. I don't know how I missed it, but I've always wondered how the Hebrew people ended up in Egypt and enslaved by Pharaoh. Joseph, at the end of Genesis, was sold by his jealous brothers to traders. He was then purchased by an Egyptian officer. You've got to read it! Exodus 1 tells the story of how and why Israelites became enslaved. A must-read as well.

Included in Exodus is the story of Moses, born into a Hebrew family but adopted by the Pharaoh's daughter and raised in the royal household. When he grew up, Moses learned of his true heritage and felt called by God to lead his people out of Egypt to freedom. With God's help, Moses was able to perform miracles and send out plagues, convincing the Pharaoh to release the Israelites from slavery. The Israelites then fled Egypt, crossing the Red Sea with the help of God. They then spent forty years wandering the desert before finally reaching God's Promised Land.

Exodus also contains the Ten Commandments, which God gave to Moses on Mount Sinai as a guide for how the Israelites should live (Exodus 20:3-17).

3. Leviticus

Leviticus primarily deals with ancient Israel's religious and moral laws. It contains instructions on how to build the Arc of the Covenant/Tabernacle, how to offer sacrifices, how to purify oneself, and how to maintain personal and community hygiene during that time.

The book also outlines the roles and responsibilities of the priests and Levites who carried out the religious rituals. While some laws may seem outdated or irrelevant today, Leviticus provides valuable insight into ancient Israel's religious practices and cultural norms.

It was through reading Leviticus that I understood why Jesus's blood had to be shed for our sins. Throughout the book of Leviticus, animal sacrifices are made to God with their blood being splattered on an altar. Jesus was that blood sacrifice for us! "...without the shedding of blood there is no forgiveness of sins," (Hebrews 9:22, ESV - Eastern Standard Version).

4. Numbers

Numbers mainly discusses the Israelites' journey from Mount Sinai to the plains of Moab, right before the Promised Land.

The book of Numbers gets its name from the two censuses taken at the beginning and the end of the Israelites' journey. It also covers the laws and regulations, given to the Israelites by God through Moses and Aaron, and the struggles and challenges they faced along the way.

The book of Numbers teaches us about obedience, faithfulness, and God's provision and protection over his people. Also, read Numbers 11:5 to know what Christians are jokingly referring to when they say, "They long for leeks and onions!"

5. Deuteronomy

Deuteronomy contains a series of speeches given by Moses to the Israelites before they entered the Promised Land. The book is essentially a restatement of the laws given to the Israelites in the previous books of the Bible, along with some additional laws and instructions.

One of the main themes of Deuteronomy is the idea of covenant—the relationship between God and his people. The book emphasizes the importance of following God's laws and commands, and the blessings that come with obedience. It also warns of the consequences of disobedience, such as punishment and exile. Deuteronomy can offer valuable lessons on personal responsibility and the importance of choosing to follow God's ways. It can also provide insight into the history and culture of ancient Israel and how their laws and beliefs shaped their society.

Have you ever wondered why debts fall off your credit report after seven years? It's in the Bible! "At the end of every seventh year you must cancel the debts of everyone who owes you money," (Deuteronomy 15:1, NLT).

6. Joshua

Joshua tells the story of how the Israelites, led by Joshua, conquered the land of Canaan as God had promised them. It's a story of faith, courage, and obedience to God. The book shows how God keeps his promises and leads his people to victory. It also teaches us the importance of following God's commands and trusting him to guide us.

In the last chapter of Joshua, God reminds the tribes of Israel that he gave them land they did not toil, cities they didn't build, and that they live in them and eat from vineyards and olive groves that they did not plant! The people are then asked who they will serve (Joshua 24:15). "Therein is the popular scripture I'm sure you've likely seen on wall art: 'But as for me and my household, we will serve the Lord.'"

7. Judges

Judges covers the period of Israel's history from the death of Joshua to the rise of the monarchy. During this time, the Israelites were led by a series of judges who were raised up by God to deliver them from their enemies and to keep them faithful to him.

The book contains many exciting stories, including the famous story of Samson and Delilah (Delilah tricked Samson into disclosing the source of his power) and the story of Deborah and Barak (who fought a battle to save Israel). The book also serves as a warning against the dangers of idolatry, as the Israelites repeatedly fall into this sin and suffer the consequences. Idolatry is extreme admiration, love, or reverence for something . . . other than God!

Overall, the book of Judges is a fascinating account of a turbulent period in Israel's history, and it offers valuable lessons about obedience to God and the dangers of turning away from him.

8. Ruth

The book of Ruth tells of a woman named Ruth who was widowed at a young age. She chooses to stay with her mother-in-law, Naomi, who is also widowed. Ruth accompanies Naomi back to her homeland of Bethlehem. There, Ruth meets and marries a man named Boaz, becoming an ancestor of King David. The book teaches the importance of loyalty, kindness, and family, and is often read during the Jewish holiday of Shavuot.

In today's culture, a woman may say she is looking for her "knight in shining armor!" In the days of Ruth, she would be "looking for her Boaz!" Do you want to know why? Read the book of Ruth!

9. 1 Samuel

The book of 1 Samuel (First Samuel) is a fascinating portrayal of the rise of Israel's monarchy. It tells the story of Samuel, the last of Israel's judges, who anoints Saul as Israel's first king. However, Saul fails to obey God. The Lord then sought out a man after his own heart, eventually replacing Saul with David. David became Israel's greatest king.

The book features themes such as obedience, faithfulness, and the consequences of sin, as well as exciting battles and political intrigue. It's an engaging read for anyone interested in history, religion, or literature.

10. 2 Samuel

2 Samuel (Second Samuel) continues the story of David, who becomes king of Israel after the death of Saul. The book covers David's reign, including his victories in battle, his personal life, and the challenges he faced as a ruler. It also includes the story of David's affair with Bathsheba and the consequences that followed. Overall, the book of 2 Samuel provides insight into the life of one of Israel's most famous kings and the struggles he faced as a leader. Yet, with all of David's shortcomings, he is still considered "a man after God's own heart!" Read the book to find out why.

11. 1 Kings

1 Kings (First Kings) tells the story of the kings of Israel and Judah after the death of King David. It covers about 120 years and focuses on the reign of Solomon (King David's son), who built the Temple in Jerusalem, and his successors. The book deals with issues such as the division of the kingdom after Solomon's reign, the rise and fall of various kings, and the importance of obedience to God's laws. It also includes stories of the prophets Elijah and Elisha, who performed miracles and spoke out against the idolatry of the times.

12. 2 Kings

2 Kings (Second Kings) covers the period from the reign of King Ahaziah to the fall of Jerusalem and Babylonian captivity. The book highlights the importance of following God's commandments and the consequences of disobedience. It also includes many miraculous events and teachings. 2 Kings is a fascinating and insightful account of the history of Israel and God's plan for his people.

13. 1 Chronicles

1 Chronicles (First Chronicles) is a historical account of the lineage of the Israelites from Adam to King David. The book begins with a genealogy, or family tree, which starts with Adam and goes all the way down to the return of the exiles from Babylon. It also covers the reign of King David, including his victories in battles and his preparations for the construction of the Temple in Jerusalem. The book emphasizes the importance of the Temple and the worship of God, highlighting the Levites' role in the religious life of the Israelites.

14. 2 Chronicles

2 Chronicles (Second Chronicles) tells the history of the kings of Judah (the southern kingdom of Israel) from the reign of King Solomon to the Babylonian exile. Unlike the books of Kings I & II, which cover the northern and southern kingdoms, Chronicles focuses only on Judah. The book highlights the role of the Temple and the Levites in worship, as well as the significance of prayer and repentance. 2 Chronicles offers a valuable perspective on the history of Israel and the importance of faith and obedience.

15. Ezra

Ezra is a historical book. It tells the story of the Jews who returned from exile in Babylon to Jerusalem and their efforts to rebuild the Temple. Ezra himself was a Jewish priest and scribe who led one of the groups of exiles back to Jerusalem. The book of Ezra is a fascinating account of the struggles and triumphs of the Jewish people as they sought to rebuild their homeland and reestablish their faith. It's an important book for anyone interested in Jewish history and the history of the ancient Near East.

16. Nehemiah

The book of Nehemiah tells the story of a Jewish man who is given permission by the Persian king to rebuild the walls of Jerusalem that were destroyed by the Babylonians. Nehemiah faces many challenges, including opposition from neighboring tribes and internal conflicts among the Jewish people. Despite these obstacles, he remains determined to complete his mission and restore the city to its former glory. Nehemiah emphasizes the importance of faith, prayer, and leadership, making it a valuable read for anyone looking to learn about perseverance and dedication to a cause.

17. Esther

Esther is a fascinating story about a young Jewish woman who became queen of Persia. She saved her people from destruction. The story takes place during the reign of King Ahasuerus, who threw a lavish party to show off his wealth and power. When Queen Vashti refused to obey his command to appear before him, she was banished, and a search for a new queen began. Esther, a beautiful Jewish woman, was chosen as the new queen, but she kept her Jewish identity a secret.

Meanwhile, Haman, an evil advisor to the king, plotted to exterminate all the Jews in Persia. Esther's cousin Mordecai discovered the plot and urged Esther to reveal her identity and plead for her people's lives. Esther bravely approached the king and revealed her Jewish heritage, ultimately convincing him to stop Haman's plan.

The story of Esther is a powerful example of how even the smallest and seemingly insignificant people can make a difference in the world. It is a reminder of the importance of standing up for what is right, even in the face of danger and opposition.

18. Job

The book of Job (pronounced with a long O) tells the story of a man named Job who goes through a series of trials and tribulations. Job is a wealthy man, blessed with a loving family and a successful career. However, Satan challenges God by saying Job only loves God because of his good fortune. God allows Satan to test Job's faithfulness by taking away his wealth, children, and health.

Despite his suffering, Job remains faithful to God and refuses to curse him. His friends come to comfort him, but they blame him for his problems, saying he must have done something to deserve them. Job argues with his friends and ultimately questions God, demanding an explanation for his suffering. In the end, God appears to Job and rebukes his friends for their lack of understanding. God restores Job's wealth and blesses him with a new family.

The book of Job is a powerful exploration of the problem of suffering and the nature of God's justice. It teaches us to trust in God even when we don't understand why we are suffering.

19. Psalms

Psalms is a collection of 150 religious poems or songs written by various authors throughout the history of Israel, covering a wide range of experiences and emotions, from joyful praise and thanksgiving to deep despair and sorrow.

King David wrote many psalms reflecting his personal experiences and relationship with God. Others were written by different authors, including Asaph, the son of Korah and Solomon.

The book of Psalms is often used in both Jewish and Christian worship, as the Psalms express a wide variety of feelings and experiences that people can relate to. They offer comfort, encouragement, hope, and a way to express our feelings to God. It can be an excellent resource for understanding the depth and complexity of human emotions, as well as for connecting with God in a personal and meaningful way.

My daughter Jay's favorite scripture is found in Psalms. Psalms 46:10 says, "Be still and know that I am God. I will be exalted among the nations; I will be exalted in the earth." This often comes to her mind when she needs reassurance that God is real and ever-present. Perhaps it can do the same for you.

20. Proverbs

Proverbs is a collection of advice and wise sayings that can guide you daily, covering many topics, such as relationships, work, money, and morality; many of which were written by King Solomon. Proverbs is an excellent resource for those seeking guidance on living a good and fulfilling life. The book encourages readers to seek wisdom and understanding and to make good choices that will lead to success and happiness. It also warns against foolishness and emphasizes the consequences of bad decisions. It is often recommended to read a chapter of Proverbs each day of the month, as there are thirty-one chapters.

21. Ecclesiastes

Ecclesiastes speaks to the meaning of life. It was written by King Solomon, who was known for his wisdom and wealth. The book discusses the futility of seeking pleasure, wealth, and power, as these things are temporary and do not bring true satisfaction or happiness. Instead, the author encourages us to find joy in our work, to enjoy the simple pleasures of life, and to trust in God. The book of Ecclesiastes teaches us that life is short and that we should make the most of our time while keeping an eternal perspective.

22. Song of Solomon

The Song of Solomon (in some translations "Song of Songs") is a beautiful and romantic book. It tells the story of a man and a woman deeply in love. The book is filled with passionate and poetic language that describes their love for each other.

The book is often interpreted as an allegory of God's love for his people, with the man representing God and the woman representing the people of Israel. However, it can also be read as a celebration of human love and sexuality. It is a refreshing and uplifting read. It celebrates the beauty of love and intimacy between two people. It can serve as a reminder of the importance of healthy relationships.

23. Isaiah

Isaiah is a collection of prophecies, or messages from God, delivered by the prophet Isaiah. It is divided into two main sections: chapters 1-39, which focus on the judgment of God against Israel and other nations, and chapters 40-66, which offer comfort and hope for God's people.

The book of Isaiah is challenging to read. It contains a lot of poetic language and references to historical events that might not be familiar to you. However, it offers a unique glimpse into the character of God and his plans for humanity. Some of the most famous passages in the book of Isaiah include the prophecy of the coming Messiah in chapter 9, the suffering servant in chapter 53, and the promise of a new heaven and new earth in chapters 65-66.

24. Jeremiah

Jeremiah is a prophetic book. It tells the story of Jeremiah, a prophet called by God to deliver his message to the people of Judah during a time of great political turmoil. Jeremiah's message was one of warning, urging the people to turn away from their sinful ways or face God's wrath. The book is filled with prophecies of impending doom and destruction, but it also contains messages of hope and restoration for those who listen to God's call. It is a relevant and thought-provoking read, dealing with themes of personal responsibility, faith, and the consequences of one's actions.

It just so happens that my favorite scripture, as well as my daughter Jazmine's favorite scripture, are both in this book. Jeremiah 29:11 is mine, reminding me that God wants peace and well-being for me. Jeremiah 29:13 is Jazmine's favorite, reminding her to seek him, and providing assurance that he will make himself known to her when she does! Read the scriptures to see why!

25. Lamentations

Lamentations is a collection of five poems that mourn Jerusalem's destruction and its people's suffering. It was written by the prophet Jeremiah, who witnessed the destruction firsthand. The poems express deep sorrow and grief, but they also offer hope and a call to repentance. The book reminds us of the consequences of sin and the importance of turning to God in times of trouble. Despite its somber tone, the book of Lamentations offers valuable lessons and insights for anyone seeking to increase their faith and understanding of God's love and mercy.

26. Ezekiel

Ezekiel is one of the prophetic books of the Bible, written by the prophet Ezekiel. It contains a series of visions and prophecies that Ezekiel received from God, along with some historical events that took place during his lifetime. The book can be divided into three main sections; the judgment on Israel, the judgment on the nations, and the restoration of Israel.

In the first section, God pronounces judgment on the Israelites for their disobedience and idolatry. Ezekiel is told to perform several symbolic acts to illustrate the coming judgment, such as lying on his side for a certain number of days and cooking bread over human waste. Understanding the historical significance of these acts will require further research on your part.

In the second section, God pronounces judgment on the surrounding nations for their mistreatment of Israel. This section includes prophecies against nations such as Egypt, Babylon, and Tyre.

Finally, in the third section, God promises to restore Israel and bring the Israelites back to their land. This section includes some of the most well-known prophecies in the book, such as The Prophecy of the New Temple and The Valley of Dry Bones.

The book of Ezekiel can be a challenging read. Still, it provides a powerful reminder of God's justice, his sovereignty, and his faithfulness to his people.

27. Daniel

The book of Daniel is a collection of stories and prophecies about a Jewish man named Daniel and his experiences while living in Babylonian captivity. It's divided into two main parts: the first half contains stories about Daniel and his three friends, while the second half includes prophecies about future events.

The stories in the first half include Daniel and his friends being taken to Babylon, where their names were changed to Babylonian names: Daniel was given the name Belteshazzar, Hananiah was given the name Shadrach, Mishael was given the name Meshach, and Azariah was given the name Abednego. They were trained to serve in the king's court. When they refused to worship a golden statue, they were thrown into a fiery furnace, but they miraculously survived!

The prophecies in the second half of the book include dreams and visions that Daniel receives from God, which reveal future events such as the rise and fall of various empires, the coming of a powerful king, and the ultimate triumph of God's kingdom. The book of Daniel teaches significant lessons about faith, obedience, and trust in God, even in difficult circumstances.

28. Hosea

The book of Hosea is named after its author, the prophet Hosea. It contains fourteen chapters and is written in a poetic style. The book tells the story of Hosea's marriage to a woman named Gomer, who was unfaithful. Through this story, Hosea illustrates how the Israelites had been unfaithful to God by worshiping other gods and engaging in immoral behavior. The book also contains messages of judgment, warning, and hope for Israel. It emphasizes the importance of remaining faithful and the consequences of turning away from God.

29. Joel

Joel is a short but powerful book. It was written by the prophet Joel and contains messages from God about the importance of repentance and the coming of judgment.

The book is divided into three chapters, beginning with a description of a devastating locust plague that destroyed the land of Judah. Joel uses this natural disaster as a metaphor for the destruction that will come upon the people if they do not turn away from their sinful ways and return to God.

The second chapter is a call to repentance, where Joel urges the people to fast (not eat and/or drink for a period of time) and pray to seek God's forgiveness. He also promises that if they do so, God will have mercy on them and restore their fortunes.

Finally, the third chapter contains a vision of the coming day of the Lord, when God will judge the nations and establish his kingdom on Earth. Joel's message is one of warning and hope, urging the people to turn away from their sins and look to God for salvation. It is a message that is just as relevant today as it was thousands of years ago.

30. Amos

Amos is a collection of prophecies and teachings from the prophet Amos, who lived in the southern kingdom of Judah during eighth century BC (before Christ).

The book of Amos is a warning to the people of Israel and Judah about their sins of injustice, oppression, and idolatry. Amos prophesies that God will punish them if they do not repent and return to him.

The book is divided into three sections. The first section contains prophecies against Israel's neighboring nations, while the second section focuses on Israel itself. The third section includes visions of judgment and restoration. The book of Amos teaches us about the importance of social justice and caring for the vulnerable and poor. It also emphasizes the need for repentance and turning back to God.

31. Obadiah

Obadiah is a short book. It is only one chapter long, but it contains an important message. The book is a prophecy about Edom, a nation known for its hostility towards Israel. The book's message is that God will bring judgment upon Edom for its violence and mistreatment of Israel. The book also contains a message of hope for Israel, as it assures them that God will protect and deliver them from their enemies. Obadiah reminds us that God is just and will hold nations accountable for their actions.

32. Jonah

Jonah is a short but profound story about a prophet named Jonah who receives a message from God to go to the city of Nineveh and preach to the people there.

However, Jonah didn't want to go because he disliked the people of Nineveh. He was also afraid they wouldn't listen to him. Instead of doing what God directed him to do, Jonah boarded a ship headed in the opposite direction in an attempt to run from God. God sent a storm, and the sailors on the ship realized the storm was because of Jonah. Eventually, they threw Jonah overboard to calm the storm. God then sent a giant fish to swallow Jonah, where he spent three days and nights before being vomited onto shore. After this experience, Jonah decided to go to Nineveh and preach to the people there. Surprisingly, they repented and turned to God, which made Jonah angry because he wanted God to punish them. The book of Jonah teaches us about God's mercy and love for all people, even those we may not like or agree with.

33. Micah

Micah was one of the twelve minor prophets in the Old Testament. Micah lived in Judah during the reigns of three kings. Micah's message is one of warning, rebuke, and hope. He condemned the corruption and social injustice of the leaders and called for repentance and a return to God. He also prophesied the coming of a future ruler who would bring peace, justice, and salvation to the people. The book of Micah is a reminder that God cares about justice and righteousness, and that we are called to live in a way that honors him. This book can help us understand the importance of social justice, the consequences of sin, and the hope we have in God's promises.

34. Nahum

Nahum is a prophetic book that contains a message of judgment against the city of Nineveh. Nineveh was a powerful city in ancient times, and it was known for its wickedness and cruelty. The prophet Nahum predicted that God would bring destruction upon the city as a punishment for its sins. This book shows that God is just and will not tolerate evil forever. It teaches us the importance of repentance and turning away from our sinful ways. The book of Nahum reminds us that God is sovereign and that he will ultimately bring justice to the world.

35. Habakkuk

Habakkuk is a short book, consisting of only three chapters. It is unique, unlike any other in the Bible, as the book records a conversation between the prophet Habakkuk and God. In the conversation, Habakkuk questions why God allows evil and injustice to exist in the world. God responds by revealing his plan to judge the wicked and vindicate the righteous. The book ends with Habakkuk's prayer of trust and confidence in God, even amid difficult circumstances.

The book of Habakkuk can be a great resource to help understand the nature of faith and how to trust in God during difficult times. It can also provide insight into how God deals with evil and injustice.

36. Zephaniah

Zephaniah is short but compelling. It contains three chapters that focus on God's judgment and salvation. Zephaniah was a prophet who spoke to the people of Judah during a time when they had turned away from God and were practicing idolatry. He warned them of the coming judgment and offered hope for those who returned to God.

The book of Zephaniah can serve as a reminder of the importance of staying faithful to God and avoiding the temptations of the world. It also highlights the themes of judgment and salvation, which are central to the Christian faith. The book encourages readers to seek God and trust in his plan for their lives.

37. Haggai

Haggai contains messages from God to the people of Israel during their time of rebuilding the Temple in Jerusalem. Haggai was a prophet who urged the people to put God first and prioritize rebuilding the Temple above their own comfort and prosperity. The book encourages the people to repent and turn back to God. It promises that if they do so, God will bless them and provide for their needs.

Haggai teaches us about the importance of putting God first in our lives and trusting in Him to provide for us.

38. Zechariah

Zechariah is a prophetic book. It is named after the prophet Zechariah, who is believed to have written it. The book contains a series of visions and prophecies given to Zechariah when the Jews were returning to Jerusalem after their exile in Babylon.

The book of Zechariah can be divided into two parts; the first part, chapters 1-8, contain eight visions that were given to Zechariah, while the second part, chapters 9-14 include a series of prophecies about the future. The book is vital to the Christian faith because it contains many Messianic prophecies that were fulfilled in Jesus Christ. For example, Zechariah 9:9 prophesied that the Messiah will enter Jerusalem on a donkey, which is exactly what Jesus did when he entered the city on Palm Sunday. It is a powerful reminder of God's faithfulness to his people, even in times of difficulty and hardship.

39. Malachi

Malachi is the last book in the Old Testament and is named after the prophet Malachi. It contains a series of messages from God to the people of Israel, particularly the priests and leaders who were not living up to their responsibilities. Malachi reminds them of their duty to honor God and follow his commandments. He also speaks about the coming of a messenger, John the Baptist, who will prepare the way for the Lord, and the day of judgment.

It is verses 3:8-12 of this book that are often quoted by pastors regarding the tithe (the first 10% of all income) being given to the church. Read the entire chapter for context.

New Testament

The New Testament is a collection of books in the Bible that tell the story of Jesus Christ and the early Christian Church. In most Bibles, text printed in RED indicates Jesus speaking. The books called Gospels teach about Jesus Christ and how his coming changed everything! The four Gospels are Matthew, Mark, Luke, and John, and they describe Jesus' life, teachings, death, and resurrection. Each Gospel offers a unique perspective on Jesus's life and teachings, and together, they provide a comprehensive portrait of his character and mission. The Gospels are at the center of the Christian faith and offer guidance and inspiration to millions of people around the world.

Other books in the New Testament provide guidance and teachings for Christians and explain the growth and spread of the early church. Together, these books offer a glimpse into the beliefs and practices of Christians and the role of Jesus Christ in their faith.

New Testament Books:

1. Matthew

Matthew is one of the four Gospels of the Bible. It was written by Matthew, a Jewish tax collector who became one of Jesus' twelve disciples.

Matthew tells the story of Jesus' life, teachings, and miracles. It emphasizes his role as the Jewish people's long-awaited Messiah, or Savior. It also highlights the importance of faith, love, and forgiveness in the Christian life. It can offer valuable insights into the teachings and life of Jesus and how they can be applied to our lives today. It can help us deepen our faith, understand the Christian worldview, and learn how to live a life of love and service to others.

2. Mark

Mark is one of the four Gospels. It tells the story of Jesus Christ, as well. This book is written in a fast-paced, action-packed style that focuses on the events of Jesus' life rather than his teachings. It is believed to be the first Gospel written and was likely intended for a Gentile audience.

One of the main themes of the book of Mark is the identity of Jesus as the Son of God. The book emphasizes Jesus' power and authority over sickness, nature, and even death. It also explores the relationship between Jesus and his followers, as well as his interactions with the religious leaders of his time.

The book of Mark is a great place to start reading the Bible, especially for someone new to the faith. It provides an engaging and accessible introduction to the life and teachings of Jesus Christ and may deepen one's understanding of the Christian faith.

3. Luke

Luke is one of the four Gospels. It was written by Luke, a physician and historian who was a companion of the Apostle Paul. Luke's Gospel is unique in that it provides a detailed account of Jesus' life, teachings, and miracles, as well as the events leading up to his death and resurrection.

The book of Luke can offer valuable insights into Jesus' teachings and how they can be applied to our lives today. It emphasizes the importance of loving and serving others, forgiveness, and humility. Luke also highlights the role of women in Jesus' ministry and the importance of social justice and caring for the poor.

Luke is another great starting point for anyone who wants to learn more about Jesus and his teachings. It provides a comprehensive account of his life and message. It can be a valuable source of inspiration and guidance.

4. John

John is one of the four Gospels. It was written by John, one of Jesus' disciples, and provides a unique perspective on Jesus' life and teachings.

One important theme in the book of John is the idea that Jesus is the Son of God and the Savior of the world. John emphasizes Jesus' divine nature and his role in bringing salvation to all people. It also contains many stories of Jesus' miracles, such as turning water into wine and healing the blind. These miracles serve as evidence of Jesus' divine power and reinforce the idea that he truly is the Son of God.

Another key theme in the book of John is the importance of faith in Jesus. John emphasizes the idea that believing in Jesus is crucial for receiving eternal life and experiencing God's love and grace. It is a powerful testament as well, to the life and teachings of Jesus Christ. It provides valuable insights into the nature of faith and the importance of living a life centered on the teachings of Jesus.

5. Acts

Acts is an exciting and action-packed book. It tells the story of the early Christian Church and how it grew and spread throughout the world. The book starts with the ascension of Jesus into heaven and the coming of the Holy Spirit on the Day of Pentecost. From there, it follows the journeys of the twelve Apostles, primarily Peter and Paul, as they preach the Gospel and perform miracles.

The book of Acts is full of adventure and drama, with stories of shipwrecks, persecution, and miraculous escapes. It also shows how the early Christians struggled with issues like how to include Gentiles in the church and how to deal with false teachers. It can be an inspiring and captivating read, showing how the early Christians lived out their faith with courage and passion. It also provides insight into how the church today can continue to spread the message of Jesus Christ to the world.

6. Romans

Romans is a letter written by the Apostle Paul to the church in Rome. It is a significant book in the New Testament, as it explains some of the most fundamental aspects of Christian theology. It offers valuable insights into the nature of sin, salvation, and grace. Paul emphasizes that we are all sinners and fall short of God's glory, but we can be justified through faith in Jesus Christ. He also talks about how we are all members of one body in Christ and should use our gifts to serve one another, not judge one another.

Romans is a powerful reminder of God's love for us and the incredible gift of salvation he offers through Jesus Christ. It's a great book to read and reflect on, especially for Christians looking to deepen their faith and understanding of the Bible.

The book of Romans is one of my favorite books of the Bible. It is filled with encouraging reminders of how much Jesus loves us. Romans 5:1-5; Romans 6:12-14; Romans 8:8-9; Romans 8:38-39; Romans 10:9… Too many to list. Read the book!

7. 1 Corinthians

1 Corinthians (First Corinthians) is a letter written by the Apostle Paul to the Christians in the city of Corinth. In this letter, Paul addresses several issues that were causing division and problems within the church.

One of the main issues that Paul addresses is the problem of disunity within the church. He urges the Corinthians to put aside their differences and work together for the sake of the Gospel. He also emphasizes the importance of love, which he describes as the greatest of all virtues in 1 Corinthians 13:4-8.

Another issue that Paul addresses is the problem of sexual immorality within the church. He reminds the Corinthians that their bodies are temples of the Holy Spirit and that they should honor God with their bodies. Paul also addresses other issues, including the role of women in the church, spiritual gifts, and the resurrection of the dead.

1 Corinthians offers lessons on how to live a life that is pleasing to God and how to deal with conflicts and problems within a community. It offers guidance on how to use our gifts and talents for the benefit of others and for the glory of God.

8. 2 Corinthians

The book of 2 Corinthians (Second Corinthians) is another letter written by the Apostle Paul to the church in Corinth. It is a follow-up to his first letter in which he addressed the church's issues and concerns. In 2 Corinthians, Paul continues to offer guidance and encouragement to the Corinthians while defending his ministry and authority.

One of the main themes of 2 Corinthians is the idea of reconciliation—both between God and humanity and between individuals. Paul stresses the importance of forgiveness and unity in the church and encourages the Corinthians to work toward these goals. Paul acknowledges his weaknesses and struggles, emphasizing that God's power is perfect in our weakness. He urges the Corinthians to rely on God's strength rather than their own and to trust in God's plan for their lives.

2 Corinthians is a book that offers valuable lessons on reconciliation, forgiveness, and humility. It reminds us of the importance of relying on God's strength and trusting in his plan, even when we face challenges and difficulties.

My son Omar lives with 2 Corinthians 4:4-7 in his heart daily, and tries to live accordingly every day: "Satan, who is the god of this world, has blinded the minds of those who don't believe. They are unable to see the glorious light of the Good News. They don't understand this message about the glory of Christ, who is the exact likeness of God. You see, we don't go around preaching about ourselves. We preach that Jesus Christ is Lord, and we ourselves are your servants for Jesus' sake. For God who said, 'Let there be light in the darkness,' has made this light shine in our hearts so we could know the glory of God that is seen in the face of Jesus Christ. We now have this light shining in our hearts, but we ourselves are like fragile clay jars containing this great treasure. This makes it clear that our great power is from God, not from ourselves," (NLT).

9. Galatians

Galatians is a book written by the Apostle Paul to the church in Galatia. In this letter, Paul addresses a group of people trying to add certain religious practices, like circumcision, to the message of salvation through faith in Jesus Christ.

Paul emphasizes that salvation comes through faith in Jesus Christ alone, not through any human effort or works. He argues that adding these practices would only lead to legalism and a rejection of the grace of God.

The book of Galatians is essential for Christians. It also reminds us to avoid legalism and trust in God's grace rather than relying on our own efforts to earn salvation.

10. Ephesians

The book of Ephesians is also written by the Apostle Paul. It is a letter addressed to the church in Ephesus. It contains important teachings and instructions on how to live a Christian life.

One of the main themes of Ephesians is the unity of all believers in Christ Jesus. Paul emphasizes the importance of being united in faith and love. He encourages Christians to build each other up and support one another. He also stresses the importance of living a holy and righteous life, avoiding sinful behaviors.

Ephesians 6:12 holds another important theme—the idea of spiritual warfare. In this scripture, Paul reminds Christians that we are not fighting against flesh and blood but against the spiritual forces of evil. He encourages believers to put on the whole armor of God and stand firm in faith, resisting the devil and his schemes. This is my son Jr's favorite scripture because he believes, "life is not a journey we are meant to face alone. The challenges we face are too great to conquer without guidance and strength beyond ourselves. We must trust God, lean on his word, and come together as his people. Only then can we share a victory that is eternal."

My daughter Jordyn's favorite scripture is also found in the book of Ephesians. Ephesians 6:16-17 says, "In all circumstances take up the shield of faith, with which you can extinguish all the flaming darts of the evil one; and take the helmet of salvation, and the sword of the Spirit, which is the word of God," (ESV). This passage encourages her, and us all, to use the tools the Lord provides (faith, salvation and the Word of God) to fight spiritual warfare.

The book of Ephesians teaches us about the importance of living a life that is pleasing to God and the vital role that unity and support play in the Christian community.

11. Philippians

Philippians is written by the Apostle Paul to the church in Philippi. It is a letter encouraging the Philippians to live a life worthy of the Gospel and to stand firm in their faith, even during persecution and suffering.

One of the main themes of Philippians is joy. Paul writes about how we can find joy in all circumstances, even in the midst of difficult situations. He encourages us to focus on what is true, noble, right, pure, lovely, admirable, excellent, and praiseworthy, and to think about these things to experience joy.

Paul urges the Philippians to be of one mind and to work together for the sake of the Gospel. He reminds them that they are all part of the same body of Christ and that they should love and serve one another.

Philippians offers valuable lessons on finding joy and hope amid challenging circumstances and working with others toward a common goal. It also reminds us of the importance of standing firm in our faith and living a life that reflects the love of Christ.

12. Colossians

Colossians is a letter written by the Apostle Paul to the church in Colossae, a city in ancient Turkey. In the letter, Paul addresses several issues related to the Christian faith, including the nature of Christ, the role of the church, and the importance of living a holy life.

The book of Colossians can offer valuable insights into what it means to be a Christian. One of the key themes is the supremacy of Christ. Paul emphasizes that Jesus is not just a good teacher or moral example, but the Son of God and the Savior of the world. This truth has important implications for how we live our lives. We should strive to follow Christ's example and put him at the center of everything we do.

Paul encourages the Colossians to put aside their differences and work together for the sake of the Gospel. This is a lesson to Christians who may be tempted to focus on their own individual spiritual growth rather than the needs of their community.

Finally, Paul encourages the Colossians to put off their old sinful ways and put on the new self, which is created to be like God in true righteousness and holiness. This message is especially relevant. It can be easy to get caught up in the pleasures and temptations of the world. In Colossians, we are reminded that as Christians we are called to live differently and pursue a higher standard of morality (read Colossians 3:1-2 and 3:13).

You may have heard the verse Colossians 3:20, "Children obey your parents in everything, for this pleases the Lord," (NIV). Make sure you read Colossians 3:21 as well!

13. 1 Thessalonians

1 Thessalonians (First Thessalonians) is a letter written by the Apostle Paul to the church in Thessalonica. Thought to be one of the earliest books in the New Testament, it is an excellent resource for those interested in learning about the early Christian Church.

In the letter, Paul encourages the Thessalonians to continue living in a way that pleases God, especially amid persecution and opposition. He also reassures them of their hope in Christ's resurrection and return.

1 Thessalonians focuses on living a holy and pure life. Paul urges the Thessalonians to abstain from sexual immorality and to live in a way pleasing to God. He also emphasizes the importance of loving and caring for one another as a community.

Overall, the book of 1 Thessalonians offers practical advice on living a life that honors God and encourages believers to remain steadfast in their faith in the face of adversity. Read 1 Thessalonians 5:16-24

14. 2 Thessalonians

2 Thessalonians (Second Thessalonians) is another letter written by the Apostle Paul to the church in Thessalonica. In this letter, Paul addresses misunderstandings that had arisen regarding the second coming of Christ. Paul reassures the Thessalonians that the Lord has not yet returned and that they should not be deceived by false teachings or rumors.

The book of 2 Thessalonians encourages us to hold fast to our faith in Christ, even in uncertain times. It reminds us that Jesus will return one day to set everything right, and it encourages us to live in readiness for that day.

15. 1 Timothy

1 Timothy (First Timothy) is a letter written by the Apostle Paul to Timothy, a young leader in the church. In this letter, Paul provides guidance and instruction on how to lead the church and live a godly life.

One of the book's central themes is the importance of sound doctrine and teaching. Paul urges Timothy to guard against false teachings and to teach the gospel truth. He also emphasizes the importance of prayer and the need to live a life consistent with one's beliefs.

Another important topic in the book is the role of women in the church. Paul provides instructions on how women should dress and behave in public worship. He also discusses the role of women in leadership positions within the church.

The book of 1 Timothy can offer lessons on leadership, the importance of sound doctrine, and the role of women in the church. It can also serve as a reminder to live a life that is consistent with one's beliefs and to remain grounded in prayer.

16. 2 Timothy

2 Timothy (Second Timothy) is a letter written by the Apostle Paul to his young disciple, Timothy. In this letter, Paul encourages Timothy to continue in his faith and ministry, even in the face of opposition and persecution.

Paul urges Timothy to cling to the truth of the Gospel and guard against false teachings and teachers. He reminds Timothy of the importance of studying and understanding the Scriptures.

This book highlights the importance of endurance and perseverance in the Christian life. Paul speaks of his own sufferings and imprisonment for the sake of the Gospel. He encourages Timothy to be willing to endure suffering and hardship for the sake of Christ. He reminds Timothy that God has not given us a spirit of fear, but of power, love, and self-discipline.

I believe 2 Timothy 2:15-16 and 2 Timothy 3:16-17 are scriptures essential for Christian living. Read them to see why!

17. Titus

Titus is a letter written by the Apostle Paul to his disciple Titus, a leader in the early Christian Church. In this letter, Paul instructs Titus on how to lead and organize the church on Crete, an island in the Mediterranean Sea.

The book of Titus offers insights into leadership and community-building. Some key themes in the book include the importance of sound doctrine, good works, and holy living. Paul emphasizes the need for leaders to be above reproach (consistently upright) and to model Christ-like behavior. He encourages Titus to teach others to do the same (Titus 2:11-14).

Titus offers practical guidance for building a strong and healthy community of believers, and it reminds us of the importance of living out our faith in our daily lives.

18. Philemon

In this short letter written by the Apostle Paul to a man named Philemon, Paul appeals to Philemon to forgive and receive back his former slave Onesimus. Onesimus had run away and become a Christian through Paul's ministry.

The book of Philemon teaches us about the power of forgiveness and reconciliation, even in difficult circumstances. Philemon also emphasizes the equality of all believers in Christ, regardless of their social status or background. It offers valuable lessons on forgiveness, humility, and the importance of treating others with respect and dignity. It also shows us the importance of standing up for what is right and just, even if it means going against social norms or expectations.

19. Hebrews

The book of Hebrews is a letter written to Jewish Christians in the first century. The letter's author is unknown. It is believed to have been written by someone familiar with the Jewish sacrificial system and who deeply understood the teachings of Jesus.

The letter addresses Jewish Christians facing persecution and hardship, encouraging them to persevere in their faith. The author argues that Jesus is superior to the angels, Moses, and the Jewish priests, because he is the ultimate High Priest who offered himself as a sacrifice for the sins of humanity.

Hebrews emphasizes the importance of faith in Jesus and the need to persevere in the face of trials and tribulations. It also teaches that Jesus is the only way to salvation and that his sacrifice on the cross is sufficient to cleanse us of our sins.

Hebrews 5:12-6:1 reminds me that I can always do more to tell and teach others about Jesus Christ. Hebrews 12:1-2 serves as a reminder to me to do the work God has set before me by staying focused on Jesus who endured the cross for me and for you. Read the scriptures to see why!

20. James

James, a leader in the early Christian Church and likely the brother of Jesus, wrote this practical and straightforward guide for living a Christian life.

The book is about putting faith into action. James emphasizes that faith without works is dead, meaning true faith should be demonstrated through our actions and behaviors. He encourages his readers to be doers of the word, not just hearers, and to live out their faith in practical ways.

James also addresses various relevant issues for his audience, such as trials and temptations, wealth and poverty, and controlling the tongue. He emphasizes the importance of humility, patience, and wisdom. Furthermore, he encourages his readers to seek God's guidance in all areas of their lives.

The book of James provides practical advice for living a Christian life in a world that can be challenging. My favorite scriptures in James are James 1:3-8. Read them to see why!

21. 1 Peter

1 Peter (First Peter) is an integral part of the New Testament. It was written by the Apostle Peter, one of Jesus' closest disciples and a leader in the early Christian Church.

It is a letter addressed to Christians who were facing persecution and hardship. Peter encourages them to remain steadfast in their faith and offers practical advice on how to do so. Peter acknowledges that Christians will face trials and difficulties in this life, but he reminds them that their hope is in Christ and that strength and comfort can be found in Christ. He also emphasizes the importance of living a holy and upright life, even amid persecution.

Peter uses the analogy of living as strangers and aliens in this world. Peter reminds readers that they are citizens of heaven and their ultimate home is not on this earth. This perspective can be very valuable for individuals still figuring out their place in the world and for those who may feel the need to fit in.

1 Peter offers hope and encouragement for Christians. It reminds us that our ultimate hope is in Christ, that suffering is a normal part of the Christian life, and that we are called to live in ways that are "strange" or "alien" to this world.

22. 2 Peter

2 Peter (Second Peter) is a letter written by the Apostle Peter to early Christians. It is a short book, consisting of only three chapters, but it is packed with essential teachings. Peter wrote this letter to encourage Christians to remain faithful to Jesus and to warn them about false teachers spreading heresy. He also reminds his readers of the importance of living a holy and godly life, and the promise of Christ's return.

The book of 2 Peter offers guidance on navigating the challenges of living a Christian life in a world that often opposes it. It emphasizes the importance of standing firm in one's faith, being aware of false teachings, and living a life of moral excellence. It also offers hope and assurance that Jesus will return one day to establish his kingdom on Earth.

23. 1 John

1 John (First John) is a letter written by the Apostle John to a group of early Christians. It is a short book, containing only five chapters, but it holds important teachings for Christians.

One of the main themes of 1 John is the importance of love. John emphasizes that God is love, and we should love one another as God has loved us. He also stresses the importance of living a life of obedience to God's commands. He warns against false teachings and false prophets.

The book of 1 John provides comfort and assurance in knowing that we are loved by God and that we can have confidence in our relationship with him. It is an excellent reminder of the importance of love in the Christian faith; it is a call to live a life reflecting love in all we do.

24. 2 John

2 John (Second John) is a short letter written by the Apostle John to a woman and her children. The letter is a reminder to the reader to love one another and to stay true to the teachings of Jesus Christ.

John emphasizes the need to love one another in truth and warns against false teachers who deny the truth of Jesus Christ. He encourages his readers to stay faithful to the teachings they have received and to avoid anyone who tries to lead them astray.

25. 3 John

The book of 3 John (Third John) is a short letter written by the Apostle John to Gaius. In the letter, John praises Gaius for his faithfulness and hospitality towards other believers. He also warns Gaius about a man named Diotrephes who is causing problems in the church by refusing to welcome traveling teachers and spreading false accusations about John and his companions.

Despite its short length, the book of 3 John teaches important lessons about hospitality, faithfulness, and standing up against false teachings and divisive behavior. This book can serve as a reminder to always welcome and support others in faith while also being vigilant against those who seek to cause division and harm.

26. Jude

Jude is a short letter written by Jude, a servant of Jesus Christ and the brother of James. It addresses Christians facing false teachings and immoral behavior within their community. In the letter, Jude urges the Christians to remain steadfast in their faith and to fight against those who are leading them astray.

Jude begins by reminding readers of God's judgment on those who rebelled against him in the past, such as the angels who sinned and the people of Sodom and Gomorrah. He then warns them about false teachers who have infiltrated their community and are distorting the truth about Jesus Christ. These teachers deny the lordship of Jesus and engage in immoral behavior.

Jude encourages Christians to contend for the faith and to build themselves up in their most holy faith through prayer and the power of the Holy Spirit. He also advises them to show mercy to those who doubt and to save others by snatching them from the fire of judgment.

Overall, the book of Jude teaches us to remain vigilant in our faith and to stand up against false teachings and immoral behavior. It reminds us of the importance of relying on God's strength and guidance and of showing love and mercy to those who are struggling in their faith.

27. Revelation

Revelation, also known as the Apocalypse, is the final book of the Bible. It is a highly symbolic and metaphorical text that has fascinated and puzzled people for centuries. The book was written by the Apostle John, describing a series of visions he had while on the island of Patmos.

Revelation is full of vivid images and dramatic scenes, such as The Four Horsemen of the Apocalypse, The Seven Seals, and The Beast. It also contains messages of hope and encouragement for believers, as well as warnings of judgment and punishment for those who reject God.

The book of Revelation can be both exciting and challenging. It offers a glimpse into a world of spiritual warfare and cosmic conflict, and it reminds us of the ultimate victory that is possible through faith in God. At the same time, the book's symbolism and complex imagery can be difficult to decipher, and it can be easy to get lost in the details.

One helpful approach to understanding the book of Revelation is to focus on its overarching themes and messages. These include the sovereignty of God, the power of prayer, the importance of faithfulness, and the ultimate triumph of good over evil. Keeping these themes in mind, you can gain a deeper appreciation for the book's significance.

Commentaries

Commentaries of the Bible are books or online resources that provide interpretation and analysis of the Bible's text. These commentaries can be written by scholars, theologians, or other experts in the field. They can offer insight into the historical and cultural context of the Bible, as well as its theological and moral implications. Some commentaries are geared towards specific audiences, such as pastors or laypeople, while others are more academic. Overall, commentaries of the Bible are valuable resources for those seeking to deepen their understanding.

To use commentaries of the Bible, first, select a specific book of the Bible you want to study. Then, find a commentary that corresponds to that particular book. You can search for commentaries online or purchase a physical copy. When reading the commentary, pay attention to the author's interpretation of the text. It's important to remember that commentaries are written by humans and can contain biases or differing interpretations. Therefore, it's recommended to consult multiple commentaries and compare them to gain a more well-rounded understanding of the Bible text.

There are many Bible commentaries available for study. Some of the most highly regarded include:

1. Matthew Henry's Commentary: This is a classic commentary written by Matthew Henry in the eighteenth century. It provides a verse-by-verse analysis of the entire Bible.

2. The Expositor's Bible Commentary: This commentary was written by a team of evangelical scholars and provides a thorough analysis of the text.

3. The New Interpreter's Bible: This is a modern commentary series that includes contributions from a diverse group of scholars and provides historical, cultural, and literary analysis of the text.

4. The Tyndale Commentaries: This is a popular commentary series that provides a concise and accessible analysis of each book of the Bible.

5. The Anchor Yale Bible Commentary: This is a scholarly commentary series that provides an in-depth analysis of the text and includes contributions from experts in the field.

These are just a few examples of the many commentaries available for Bible study. And again, they were written by men; they are their interpretations of the Bible. Only the Bible itself was God-Inspired, meaning God gave the authors of the Bible what to write. (2 Timothy 3:16-17).

Bible Interpretations

Interpretations of the Bible refer to the various ways in which people understand and explain the meaning of the text. Scholars, theologians, and religious groups may have different interpretations depending on their beliefs, cultural backgrounds, and historical contexts. Some interpret the Bible literally, while others take a more figurative or symbolic approach.

Also, there are different methods of interpretation, including historical, literary, and theological analysis. If you belong to a church, for example, your pastors are providing their interpretation of what the Bible says. Thus, it is important that you read the Bible and study it as well to ensure that what is being taught is from the Bible, within context, and correct.

Ultimately, the goal of biblical interpretation is to gain a deeper understanding of the text and its relevance to our lives today.

Bible Translations

There are many translations of the Bible available including the King James Version (KJV), the Amplified Bible (AMP), the New Living Translation (NLT), and the New Revised Standard Version (NRSV) as a few examples. Each translation has its own style and language, but the content of the Bible remains the same across them all. Example:

KJV - John 3:16 "For God so loved the world, that he gave his only begotten Son, that whosoever believeth in him should not perish, but have everlasting life."

AMP - John 3:16 "For God so [greatly] loved and dearly prized the world, that He [even] gave His [One and] only begotten Son, so that whoever believes and trusts in Him [as Savior] shall not perish but have eternal life."

NLT - John 3:16 "For this is how God loved the world: He gave his one and only Son, so that everyone who believes in him will not perish but have eternal life."

NRSV - John 3:16 "For God so loved the world that he gave his only Son, so that everyone who believes in him may not perish but may have eternal life."

It is essential to choose a translation that you can understand and connect with personally. I grew up reading the King James Version. It was very difficult to read and understand at the time.

The New Living Translation (NLT) is often recommended as the simplest version of the Bible to understand. It uses modern language to convey the meaning of the text in a way that is easy to comprehend for modern readers. This is the translation I use most often now. However, my scripture memorizations are in the King James Version because I was taught scripture using that translation.

46

Conclusion

In summary, the most important thing for a new Christian to know about the Bible is that it is the inspired word of God and contains the teachings and instructions for how to live a fulfilling and meaningful life. God wants an intimate relationship with you. To be intimate with him, you have to know him. To know him, you have to read the Bible.

Approach the Bible with an open mind and a willingness to learn, and seek guidance from reputable commentaries and interpretations. As a new Christian, starting with the New Testament, which tells the story of Jesus and his teachings, can be very helpful. Ultimately, Christianity is a lifestyle, and the Bible is a guide to developing a personal relationship with God and following his ways, daily.

The Bible has guided me through some of the most difficult times of my life. It provided comfort, wisdom, and instruction when I needed it most. I pray it will do the same for you.

www.ingramcontent.com/pod-product-compliance
Lightning Source LLC
Chambersburg PA
CBHW071242090426
42736CB00014B/3192